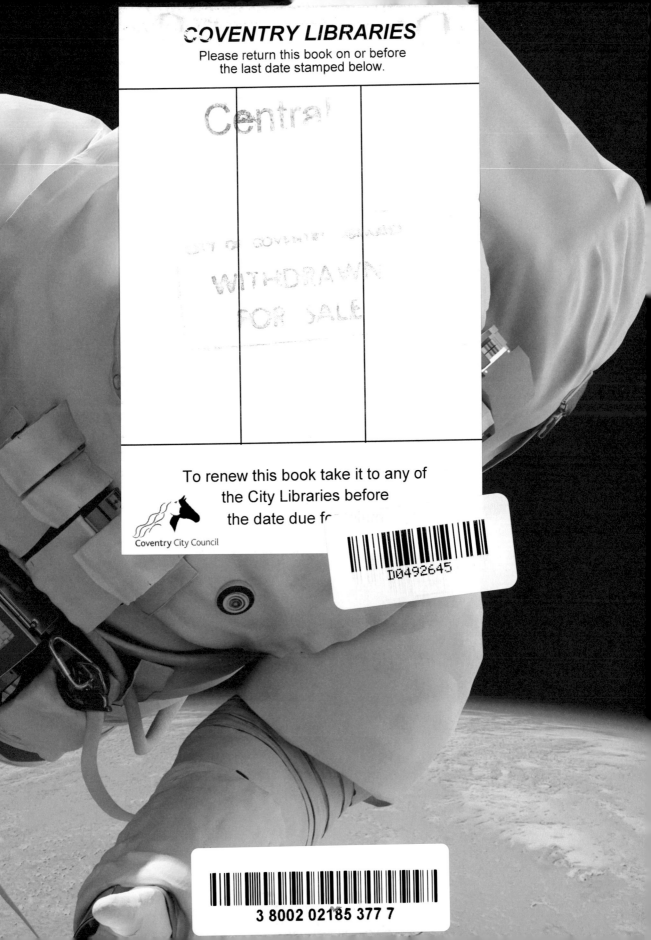

[A Maths]
JOURNEY
+ < = ~ ± ÷ ›through‹
# SP CE

CONTENTS

go figure

As the leader of a space mission to Mars, your job is to use your mathematical knowledge to get your crew to the red planet safely.

Learn about probability, estimating, angles, decimals and other mathematical principles and then use them to solve puzzles that will guide you through the perils of space exploration!

Answers to the Go Figure! challenges can be found on page 28.
Words in *italics* appear in the glossary on page 30.

You might find some of the questions in this book are too hard to do without the help of a calculator.
Ask your teacher about when and how to use a calculator.

WHAT EQUIPMENT DO YOU NEED?

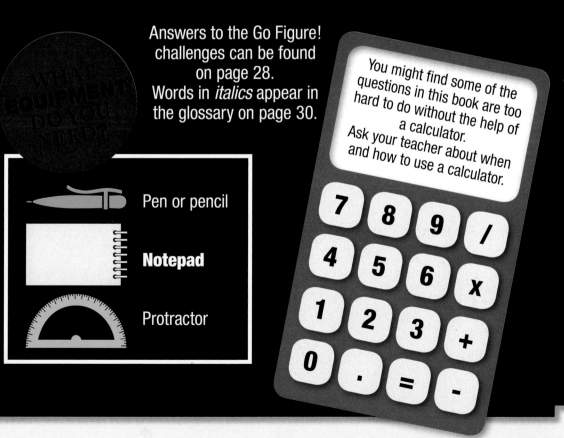

Pen or pencil

Notepad

Protractor

JOURNEY TO MARS

You are leading a mission to Mars to collect rock samples and to look for fossil evidence that there might once have been life on the planet.

LEARN ABOUT IT
ROUNDING NUMBERS AND ESTIMATING

When you make *estimates*, you need to round numbers up or down to the nearest 10, 100 or 1,000.

04

To round a number to the nearest 10, look at the figure in the units (U) column. If it is less than '5', change it to '0'.

Original number	Rounded number
H T U 213	H T U 210
341	340
904	900

If it is '5' or more, change it to '0' and increase the figure in the tens (T) column.

Original number	Rounded number
545	550
607	610
99	100

To round to the nearest hundred (H), look at the last two digits. If they are less than '50', change them to '00'. If they are equal to or more than '50', change them to '00' and increase the hundreds.

Original number	Rounded number
526	500
645	600
199	200

You can use the rounded figures to do an easy sum:

If three rockets weigh 149 tonnes, 97 tonnes and 45 tonnes, you could estimate their total weight as:
150 + 100 + 50 = 300 tonnes

⟩GO FIGURE!

You are completing some checks in your rocket before lift-off. You want to do a few rough calculations and estimates.

Mission check list

Component Check:
CHECK 1: 319 HOURS ✓
CHECK 2: 587 HOURS

Stock check: ✓
39 BOXES TEST-TUBES

Fuel check: ✓
Tank 1: 34,185 LITRES
Tank 2: 67,203 LITRES
Tank 3: 47,893 LITRES

1 One of the engineers has left a note saying he tested two components for 319 and 587 hours. Estimate the total hours to the nearest 10.

2 **You are taking 39 boxes of test-tubes. There are 256 in each box. Roughly how many will you have?**

3 Your rocket has three fuel tanks, holding 34,185 litres, 67,203 litres and 47,893 litres. Round these numbers to the nearest 1,000 and estimate how many litres of fuel there are.

3-2-1—LIFT OFF!

On the launch pad, the rocket is ready to leave and the countdown is about to begin. You need to calculate when different stages in the countdown will occur.

LEARN ABOUT IT
WORKING WITH TIME

We can tell the time using either an *analogue* clock face or with a *digital* display, which just uses numbers.

With a digital display, the time is shown using a 12-hour clock or a 24-clock. The 12-hour clock divides the day into two 12-hour cycles – one for the time from 12 midnight to 12 noon, or am, and one for the time from 12 noon to midnight, or pm. After 12 noon, you start the cycle again at 1:00 pm, until you reach 12 midnight.

For the 24-hour clock, you keep increasing the hour number beyond 12 noon. So 1:00 pm becomes 13:00, 2:00 pm becomes 14:00, and so on, until you reach 12 midnight, which starts the cycle again at 00:00.

09:30

9:30 am (12-hr) = 09:30 (24-hr)

When you *add* or subtract times, remember that there are 60 minutes in an hour. For example:

13:47 + 1 hour 35 minutes
Add the minutes first:
13:47 + 35 minutes = 14:22
Then add the hour:
14:22 + 1 hour = 15:22

15:45

3:45 pm (12-hr) = 15:45 (24-hr)

❭GO FIGURE!

Calculate the time when different stages of your rocket's countdown and mission should take place.

11:09

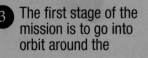

❶ The clock shows the current time – 11:09 am. The final checks on the rocket were carried out one hour and 37 minutes ago. What time were they carried out?

❷ The final countdown will start at 11:54 am and take 13 minutes. What time will it be completed?

❸ The first stage of the mission is to go into orbit around the Moon and take photographs. This stage will take 2 days and 13 hours. How many hours will it take in total?

❹ The final checks took 1 hour and 56 minutes; the countdown will take 13 minutes; it will take 7 minutes until the second engine fires. How many minutes is it from the start of final checks to the second engine firing?

OFF TO THE MOON

Your path takes you first to our own Moon. From there, you head off towards a moon orbiting Mars, called Phobos. From Phobos, you will head directly to Mars.

LEARN ABOUT IT
ANGLES

Angles are recorded in degrees (°). We measure them using a *protractor*.

08

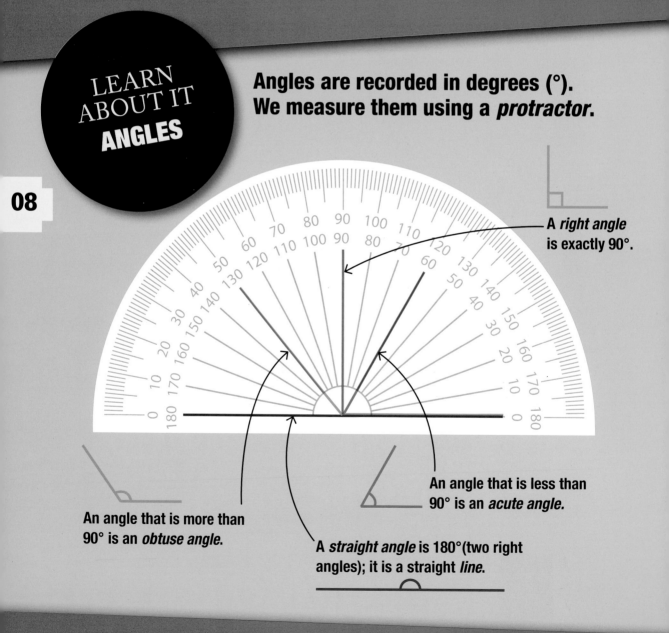

A *right angle* is exactly 90°.

An angle that is less than 90° is an *acute angle*.

An angle that is more than 90° is an *obtuse angle*.

A *straight angle* is 180°(two right angles); it is a straight *line*.

⟩GO FIGURE!

Plotting your course from Earth, to the Moon, to Phobos and then to Mars creates a path that looks like this. There is also a comet passing Mars at the same time.

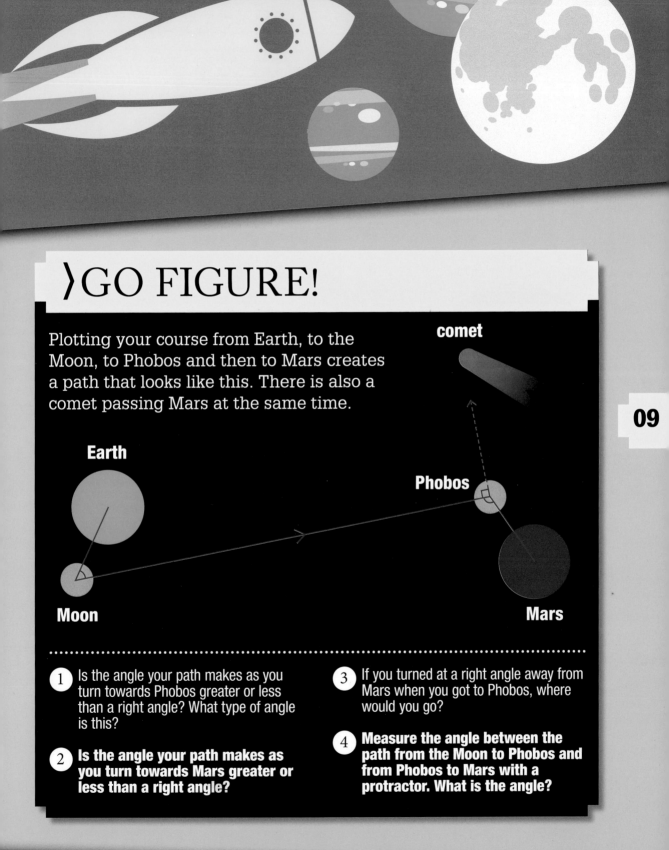

comet

Earth

Phobos

Moon

Mars

1. Is the angle your path makes as you turn towards Phobos greater or less than a right angle? What type of angle is this?

2. Is the angle your path makes as you turn towards Mars greater or less than a right angle?

3. If you turned at a right angle away from Mars when you got to Phobos, where would you go?

4. Measure the angle between the path from the Moon to Phobos and from Phobos to Mars with a protractor. What is the angle?

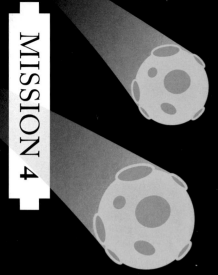

ASTEROID WATCH!

You fly through a storm of asteroids and decide to monitor them. Two astronauts count groups of asteroids from the windows on the left and on the right.

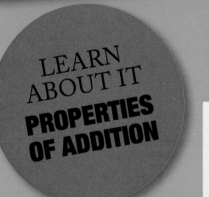

LEARN ABOUT IT

PROPERTIES OF ADDITION

There are a few rules that can help you to get the right answer when you add numbers together.

When you add 0 to a number, the number stays the same:

8 + 0 = 8

This is called the *identity property* of addition.

It does not matter which order the numbers are written down in – the sum is still the same:

12 + 11 = 11 + 12 = 23

This is the *commutative property* of addition.

You can add numbers in different groups and then add the groups together. It does not matter which order you add them in:

10 + 11 + 12 + 13 = (10 + 11) + (12 + 13) = 21 + 25 = 46

This is the same as writing:

(13 + 10) + (12 + 11) = 23 + 23 = 46

This is the *associative property* of addition.

❯GO FIGURE!

The two astronauts note down the asteroid groups as they fly past. These are the figures.

Asteroid groups

	Left window	Right window
10:00 am	6+2	2+6
10:15 am	7+0	7
10:30 am	(5+2)+1	5+(2+1)
10:45 am	4+3+1	(2+2)+3+1

1. At 10:00 am, did the astronauts record the same total number of asteroids?

2. **At 10:15 am, one astronaut missed a group of very small asteroids. Is his total the same as the other astronaut's total?**

3. At 10:30 am, did the astronauts record the same total number of asteroids?

4. **At 10:45 am, one astronaut thought there was one big and two smaller groups, but the other thought there were four small groups. Did they count the same number of large asteroids?**

5. Which of these questions show the commutative property of addition? Which shows the identity property of addition?

NEARLY THERE?

The trip recorder on your spaceship shows distances in AU – Astronomical Units. An Astronomical Unit is the distance from the Sun to Earth.

LEARN ABOUT IT
DECIMALS

One way of working with *decimal* numbers is to use a *number line*, dividing the whole numbers into ten smaller parts. This makes it easy to add and subtract decimals.

These rockets are zooming along a path that is 1.5 AU long. The path has been divided into smaller parts, with each part showing 0.1 AU.

The blue rocket is 6 marks from the start, so it has travelled 0.6 AU. The red rocket is 0.8 AU from the start. The green rocket has travelled 1.3 AU. It is 0.5 AU ahead of the red rocket. We can convert these measurements into sums:

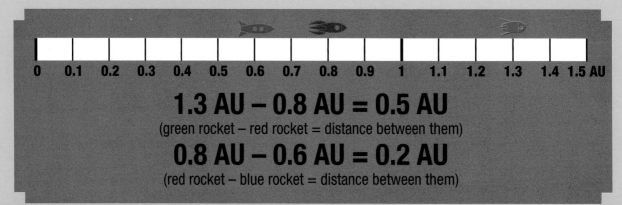

0 0.1 0.2 0.3 0.4 0.5 0.6 0.7 0.8 0.9 1 1.1 1.2 1.3 1.4 1.5 AU

$$1.3 \text{ AU} - 0.8 \text{ AU} = 0.5 \text{ AU}$$
(green rocket – red rocket = distance between them)

$$0.8 \text{ AU} - 0.6 \text{ AU} = 0.2 \text{ AU}$$
(red rocket – blue rocket = distance between them)

〉GO FIGURE!

The image below shows the position of the spaceship in relation to the Sun and the planets. There are marks at every 0.1 AU.

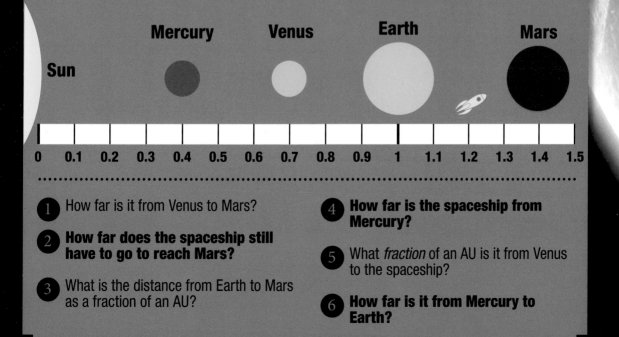

1. How far is it from Venus to Mars?

2. **How far does the spaceship still have to go to reach Mars?**

3. What is the distance from Earth to Mars as a fraction of an AU?

4. **How far is the spaceship from Mercury?**

5. What *fraction* of an AU is it from Venus to the spaceship?

6. **How far is it from Mercury to Earth?**

ASTRONAUTS HARD AT WORK

It is hard to keep track of working time in space because there is no difference between day and night. The crew have kept logs of how many hours they worked at a time.

We can compare numbers using three symbols: '<', '>' and '='. They are useful in *equations*.

14

'<' means that the total on the left side of the equation is less than the total on the right: **2 + 1 < 5.** So 2 + 1 = 3, which is less than 5.

'>' means that the total on the left side of the equation is greater than the total on the right: **4 − 1 > 1.** So 4 − 1 = 3, which is greater than 1.

'=' means that the total on the left side of the equation is equal the total on the right: **2 + 5 = 7.** So 2 + 5 is equal to 7.

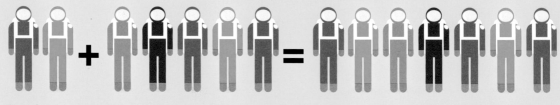

The first two symbols ('<' and '>') are called *symbols of inequality*. Mathematicians use them when they do not need to calculate the exact answer.

〉GO FIGURE!

The crew are not allowed to work more than 40 hours in a week. You have to check the time logs they have recorded.

ASTRONAUT	HOURS WORKED	MAXIMUM HOURS PER WEEK
Taylor	4 x 7 hours + 1 x 9 hours	40 hours
Jed	3 x 9 hours + 1 x 8 hours + 2 x 4 hours	40 hours
Sara	5 x 8 hours	40 hours
Karmel	1 x 5.5 hours; 1 x 7.5 hours; 1 x 9 hours; 1 x 8 hours; 1 x 6.5 hours	40 hours
Carl	3 x 8 hours + 1 x 6.5 hours + 1 x 8.5 hours	40 hours

1 In your notepad, work out the number of hours each astronaut has worked and then use the correct symbol to show whether they have worked less than, more than or equal to the maximum number of allowed hours.

2 Carl and Jed were both working on the same project. Use the right symbol to compare the time they both spent on the project.

COMET ALERT!

You have spotted several comets from outside the Solar System and tracked their courses.

LEARN ABOUT IT
LINES AND PATHS

A line represents a path in a particular direction. Lines go on forever, but they can be divided into smaller parts, called segments.

16

Lines that go in the same direction, with a fixed distance between them, are *parallel*. They will never meet.

If two lines are *perpendicular*, there is a right angle between them.

If two lines are *intersecting*, they cross. There can be any angle between the lines where they meet.

Lines (shown in maths by arrows at both ends) go on forever.

A *line segment* has two endpoints: a start and a finish.

A *ray* has one endpoint and goes on forever.

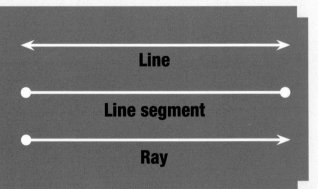

Line

Line segment

Ray

〉GO FIGURE!

It is important that your spaceship does not crash into a comet, but it can pass through the tail, which is just gas. This image shows the paths of your spaceship and the comets.

1. Which two comets are on parallel paths?

2. **Which comet is on a path perpendicular to comet B?**

3. Which paths will intersect?

4. **The spaceship will intersect the tail of a comet. Which one?**

5. Is each of these a line, a line segment or a ray?
   a) The spaceship's path from Earth to Mars.
   b) A beam of light travelling from the Sun into space.

SPACE SUPPERS

All the food that the astronauts will eat on the journey to and from Mars is stored on the spaceship.

LEARN ABOUT IT
PIE CHARTS

A *pie chart* is a good way of showing the relative sizes of bits of data. The circle is divided into slices and the size of each slice reflects the size of the data.

18

This chart shows whether astronauts prefer to train by running or cycling.

17   22

The total number of astronauts asked was 22 + 17 = 39. Of that group, 22 preferred to cycle and 17 preferred to run.

This table records the nationalities of 60 astronauts:

USA	17
Russia	23
China	13
Europe	7
	60

It is easy to see that more come from Russia than any other region. Only seven come from Europe. You can show the amounts of each entry as a fraction of the total number. These are $7/60$ (Europe), $17/60$ (USA), $23/60$ (Russia) and $13/60$ (China).

>GO FIGURE!

You want to keep track of what has been eaten on the mission and you have drawn a pie chart showing the percentages of the different meals.

CHICKEN AND RICE (40%)

BEEF AND VEGETABLES (10%)

VEGETABLE PASTA (20%)

FISH AND NOODLES (30%)

1 Which has been the most popular type of meal?

2 What percentage of the meals eaten were vegetarian pasta?

3 Put the meals in order, from the most popular to the least popular.

4 Draw your own pie chart to show which drinks the astronauts prefer. tea 2; coffee 3; hot chocolate 5

TOUCH DOWN

Your spaceship is making the final descent to Mars. You are looking for number patterns in your data as you get closer to the surface.

Sometimes, sequences of numbers make patterns. Using number lines helps to show these patterns.

LEARN ABOUT IT

NUMBER PATTERNS

20

This sequence shows what happens when you start at zero and add two each time:

0, 2, 4, 6, 8, 10...

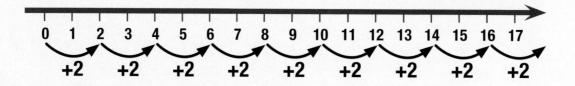

Working backwards, this sequence shows what happens when you subtract three each time, starting at 30:

30, 27, 24, 21, 18...

The next number will be 18 − 3 = 15; the number after that is 15 − 3 = 12.

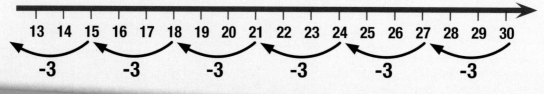

This sequence shows what happens when you double a number at each stage, starting at two:

2, 4, 8...

The next number will be 8 x 2 = 16.

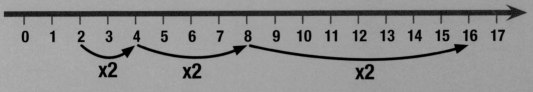

⟩GO FIGURE!

You are recording the height and temperature as you descend. You are also photographing the surface of Mars as you approach.

Mission check list

Height of spaceship:

75KM, 70KM, 65KM, 60KM...

Temperature:

0°, 1°, 3°, 6°, 10°...

Area covered:

64 KM², 32 KM², ...KM²,
8 KM², 4 KM², 2 KM²

1. You are recording the height of the spaceship every 30 seconds. The readings are 75 km, 70 km, 65 km, 60 km. What will the next reading be?

2. **It gets warmer as you move towards the sunny side of Mars. The readings are 0°, 1°, 3°, 6°, 10°. What will the next reading be?**

3. You have been photographing the surface. The area covered by each photograph decreases as you get closer, but you forgot to fill in one of the numbers. What should it be? 64 km², 32 km², __ km², 8 km², 4 km², 2 km² .

RANGING ROVERS

Your spaceship has landed on Mars. On the rocky surface, you find robotic wheeled probes, called rovers, sent from Earth in the past. Two have broken down, but another two are still moving.

LEARN ABOUT IT

MULTIPLYING AND DIVIDING WITH DECIMALS

22

When you work with decimals, it is important to remember that the numbers get smaller with each position after the decimal point, so: 0.001 is smaller than 0.01

The position after the decimal point shows tenths (T), the one after that shows hundredths (H) and the one after that shows thousandths (Th).

T H Th
0.005

To multiply a decimal number by 10, you can simply move the decimal point to the right one place. To multiply by 100, you can move it two places to the right and to multiply by 1,000, you can move it three places to the right.

x10   x100   x1,000

1.109 11.09 110.9 1109.0

To divide a decimal number by 10, you can simply move the decimal point to the left one place. To divide by 100, you can move it two places to the left and to multiply by 1,000, you can move it three places to the left.

÷10   ÷100   ÷1,000

201.4 20.14 2.014 0.2014

〉GO FIGURE!

Each rover has recorded information about its activity, storing data on how far it has travelled and how quickly it moved.

ROVER	LANDED	STOPPED ROVING	DISTANCE TRAVELLED	AVERAGE SPEED, KM/DAY
Sojourner	4 July 1997	27 September 1997	0.1 km	0.001 km/day
Spirit	4 January 2004	26 January 2010	7.7 km	0.003 km/day
Opportunity	25 January 2010	Still going	86.8 km	0.03 km/day
Curiosity	6 August 2012	Still going	5.0 km	0.002 km/day

1 Which rover is the quickest?

2 **Which rover is the slowest?**

3 How many days did it take *Opportunity* to travel 6 km?

4 **How long will it take *Curiosity* to travel a further 1 km?**

5 How far could *Spirit* travel in 15 days?

BOXES READY

You have some boxes that you want to use to package the rock samples you collect from the surface. They have been flat-packed so that they take up less room in the spaceship.

24

A flat shape that can be folded into a three-dimensional (3-D) shape is called a *net*.

Each part of the surface of the net will become a *face* of the 3-D object, while each fold line will become an *edge*, and each corner will become a *vertex*.

The net for a *cube* is made up of six squares. They do not need to be arranged like this – there are 11 different nets for a cube!

The net for a square *prism*, or cuboid, also has six faces, and looks like this:

The shapes of the faces show how the 3-D object will look. This one has triangles to make a *pyramid*:

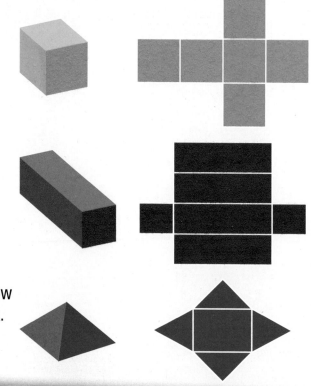

Some shapes have curved surfaces. One face of a cone is a circle; you have to bend the long surface around it.

A cylinder has two circular faces and a rectangular face that wraps around them.

〉GO FIGURE!

You have collected some specially shaped rock samples – your job is to match each one to the correct flat-packed box.

Flat-pack boxes

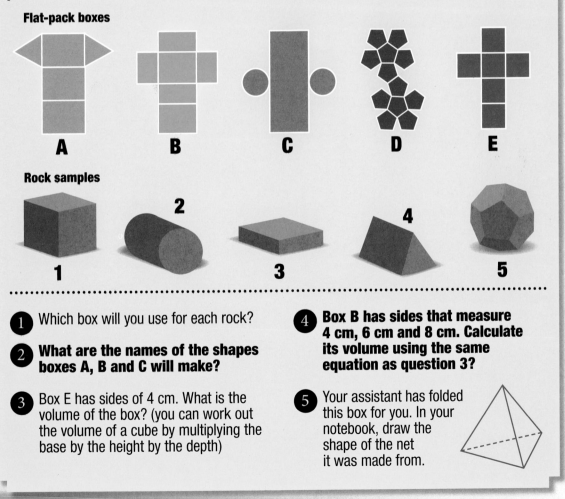

A B C D E

Rock samples

1 2 3 4 5

1 Which box will you use for each rock?

2 **What are the names of the shapes boxes A, B and C will make?**

3 Box E has sides of 4 cm. What is the volume of the box? (you can work out the volume of a cube by multiplying the base by the height by the depth)

4 **Box B has sides that measure 4 cm, 6 cm and 8 cm. Calculate its volume using the same equation as question 3?**

5 Your assistant has folded this box for you. In your notebook, draw the shape of the net it was made from.

LIFE ON MARS

One of the scientists in your research team thinks she has found fossils of microbes in some rocks. She examined a total of 10 rocks.

LEARN ABOUT IT
PROBABILITY

26

Probability **is the likelihood or chance of something happening. It can be shown as a fraction, a decimal or as a percentage.**

If you toss a coin, there are two possible outcomes: heads or tails. The probability of getting tails is: ½, 0.5 or 50 per cent

Certain things and events are more likely to occur than others and you can arrange them against a simple scale as follows:

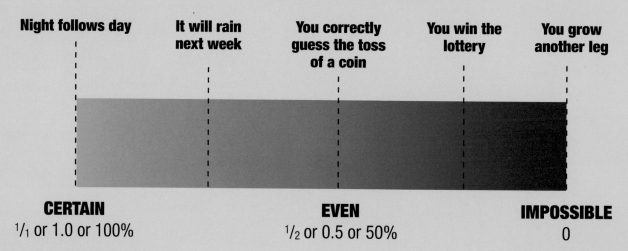

| Night follows day | It will rain next week | You correctly guess the toss of a coin | You win the lottery | You grow another leg |

CERTAIN
¹/₁ or 1.0 or 100%

EVEN
½ or 0.5 or 50%

IMPOSSIBLE
0

There are five spacesuit helmets in the airlock of your rocket, each a different size. The probability of you picking up one that fits at random is as follows:

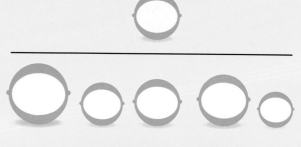

$\frac{1}{5}$ or 0.2 or 20%

〉GO FIGURE!

The rocks are spread out on a desk in front of you. Of the ten rocks, three contain fossils of microbes.

1 What is the probability of finding a fossil if you pick up a rock at random?

2 **What is the probability that the rock you pick up does not contain a fossil?**

3 The first rock you picked up did have a fossil! If you picked up another rock at random, what is the possibility that this next rock has a fossil?

4 **What is the probability that this next rock does not contain any fossil evidence?**

GO FIGURE! ANSWERS

04-05 Journey to Mars
1. 320 + 590 = 910
2. 40 x 300 = 12,000
3. 34,000 + 67,000 + 48,000 = 149,000

06-07 3-2-1–Lift off!
1. 11:09 am – 37 minutes = 10:32 am
10:32 am – 1 hour = 9:32 am or 09:32
2. 11:54 + 13 minutes = 12:07pm or 12:07
3. 2 days = 2 x 24 = 48 hours,
so 48 + 13 = 61 hours
4. 1 hr 56 mins + 13 mins + 7 mins =
1 hr 56 mins + 20 mins = 2 hrs 16 mins

28

08-09 Off to the Moon
1. It is less than a right angle.
It is an acute angle.
2. It is more than a right angle.
It is an obtuse angle.
3. You would crash into the comet!
4. 120°

10-11 Asteroid watch!
1. Yes; 6 + 2 = 2 + 6 = 8
2. Yes; 7 + 0 = 7
3. Yes; (5 + 2) + 1 = 5 + (2 + 1) = 8
4. Yes; 4 + 3 + 1 = (2 + 2) + 3 + 1 = 8
5. Q1 shows the commutative property of
addition; Q2 shows the identity property
of addition.

12-13 Nearly there?
1. 1.4 – 0.7 = 0.7 AU
2. 1.4 – 1.2 = 0.2 AU
3. 0.4 = $^4/_{10}$ = $^2/_5$ AU
4. 1.2 – 0.4 = 0.8 AU
5. 1.2 – 0.7 = 0.5 = ½ AU
6. 1 – 0.4 = 0.6 AU

14-15 Astronauts hard at work
1. Taylor = 4 x 7 + 9 = 28 + 9 = 37 < 40 hours
Jed = 3 x 9 + 8 + 2 x 4 = 27 + 8 + 8 = 43 > 40 hours
Sara = 5 x 8 = 40 = 40 hours
Karmel = 5.5 + 7.5 + 9 + 8 + 6.5 = 36.5 < 40 hours
Carl = 3 x 8 + 6.5 + 8.5 = 39 < 40 hours

2. (3 x 9) + 8 + (2 x 4) > (3 x 8) + 6.5 + 8.5
OR 27 + 8 + 8 > 24 + 6.5 + 8.5
OR 43 > 39

16-17 Comet alert!
1. B and D
2. A
3. A and D; B and C; A and E
4. C
5. (a) line segment (c) ray

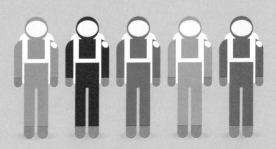

18-19 Space suppers
1. Chicken and rice
2. 20%
3. Chicken and rice (40%); fish and noodles (30%); vegetarian pasta (20%); beef and vegetables (10%)
4.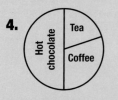

Hot chocolate | Tea | Coffee

20-21 Touch down
1. 55 km; the spaceship is descending 5 km every 30 seconds.
2. 15°; the pattern is 0 + 1; 1 + 2; 3 + 3; 6 + 4; so 10 + 5.
3. 16 km^2; the area photographed halves at each stage.

22-23 Ranging rovers
1. *Opportunity*
2. *Sojourner*
3. 6 ÷ 0.03 = 200 days
4. 1 ÷ 0.002 = 500 days
5. 15 x 0.003 = 0.045 km

24-25 Boxes ready
1. A = 4, B = 3, C = 2, D = 5, E = 1
2. A – triangular prism; B – rectangular prism or cuboid; C – cylinder
3. 4 x 4 x 4 = 64 cm^3
4. 4 x 6 x 8 = 192 cm^3
5.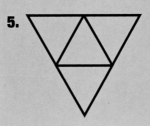

26-27 Life on Mars
1. There are ten rocks and three contain fossils, so the probability is $^3/_{10}$.
2. Seven of the ten rocks do not contain fossils, so the probability is $^7/_{10}$.
3. You have already picked up one fossil, so there are only two left and a reduced total of nine, so the probability is $^2/_9$.
4. There are still seven rocks without fossils, but a reduced total of nine, so the probability is $^7/_9$.

MATHS GLOSSARY

ACUTE ANGLE
An angle that is less than 90°.

ADD
Combining two numbers to produce
a third.

ANALOGUE
An analogue clock has a round face with
numbers and hands to point out the time.

ASSOCIATIVE PROPERTY
The associative property of addition states
that you can add up sub-groups in an
addition sum in any order and the answer
will remain the same.

COMMUTATIVE PROPERTY
The commutative property of addition
means that you can swap
numbers around in a sum and the
answer will remain the same.

CUBE
A three-dimensional shape that is
formed from six squares.

DECIMAL
Dividing whole numbers into smaller units.
One can be divided into ten decimals
(tenths), and these can be divided into ten
smaller decimals (hundredths), and so on.

DIGITAL
A digital clock only uses numbers to tell
the time.

EDGE
A line that joins two faces on a three-
dimensional object.

EQUATION
An expression that can be solved. An
equation has two sides to it that are
usually linked with an equals symbol (=),
although other symbols can be used to
show inequality between the two sides.

ESTIMATE
To produce an answer that is roughly
equivalent to the correct answer.
Estimating usually involves rounding up
or down the numbers involved.

FACE
A flat surface that forms part of a three-
dimensional object.

FRACTION
A smaller part of a whole number.
Fractions use two numbers, with one on
top of the other.

IDENTITY PROPERTY
The identity property of addition
states that if you add zero to a number,
then that number will stay the same.

INTERSECTING
When two lines cross each other. Lines
can intersect at any angle.

LINE
A straight path that goes on for ever, without a start point or an end point.

LINE SEGMENT
Part of a path with a start and an end.

NET
A flat two-dimensional shape that can be folded to create a 3-D object.

NUMBER LINE
A line that is divided into numbers and can be used to show a progression in increasing or decreasing values.

OBTUSE ANGLE
An angle that is more than 90°.

PARALLEL
When two objects or lines lie running in the same direction.

PERPENDICULAR
When two objects or lines lie at 90° or a right angle to each other.

PIE CHART
A type of chart that divides a circle into 'slices' according the proportion shown by each value. The bigger the value, the larger the slice on the pie chart.

PRISM
A three-dimensional shape that has two identical ends and flat sides.

PROBABILITY
The likelihood or chances that something will happen. Probability can be measured using fractions, percentages or decimals.

PROTRACTOR
A mathematical instrument, shaped in a circle or semi-circle. It is marked with degrees and is used to measure angles.

PYRAMID
A three-dimensional shape whose sides are formed from triangles that meet at a point above a polygon base. The base can be a triangle, square, rectangle or any shape with three or more sides.

RAY
A line that has a start point and then goes on in one direction forever.

RIGHT ANGLE
An angle of 90°.

STRAIGHT ANGLE
An angle that is 180°. This produces a straight line.

SYMBOLS OF INEQUALITY
These include the symbols '<' and '>' and show that the sum does not equal the value shown.

VERTEX
A corner on a three-dimensional object where edges meet. For example, a cube has eight vertices.

INDEX

32

WEBSITES

www.mathisfun.com
A huge website packed full of explanations, examples, games, puzzles, activities, worksheets and teacher resources for all age levels.

www.bbc.co.uk/bitesize
The revision section of the BBC website, it contains tips and easy-to-follow instructions on all subjects, including maths, as well as games and activities.

www.mathplayground.com
An action-packed website with maths games, mathematical word problems, worksheets, puzzles and videos.

ACKNOWLEDGEMENTS

First published in 2014 by Wayland
Copyright © Wayland 2014

Wayland
338 Euston Road
London NW1 3BH

Wayland Australia
Level 17/207 Kent Street
Sydney NSW 2000
All rights reserved.

Commissioning editor: Debbie Foy

Produced by Tall Tree Ltd
Editors: Jon Richards
Designer: Ed Simkins
Consultant: Steve Winney

ISBN: 9780750282390

Dewey ref: 510-dc23

10 9 8 7 6 5 4 3 2 1

Printed in China
Wayland is a division of Hachette
Children's Books, an Hachette UK company.
www.hachette.co.uk

The website addresses (URLs) included in this book were valid at the time of going to press. However, it is possible that contents or addresses may have changed since the publication of this book. No responsibility for any such changes can be accepted by either the author or the Publisher.

Picture credits
7 Shutterstock.com/amskad,
13 Shutterstock.com/sdecoret, 15 Shutterstock.com/iurii, 18tl Shutterstock.com/PremiumVector, 19t, 23t, 26tl courtesy of NASA

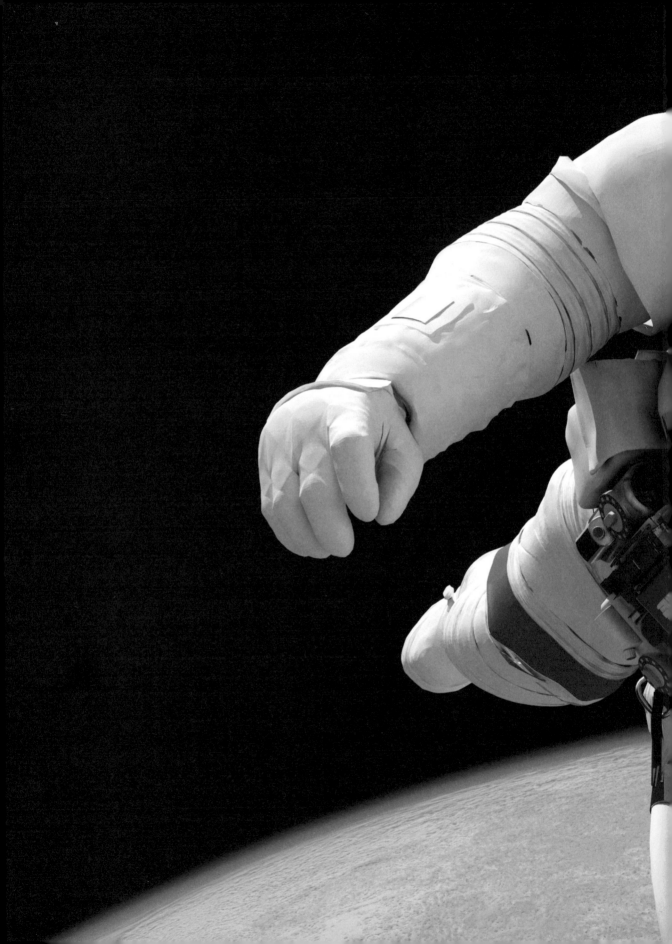